Handball Practice 11 – Extensive and diverse athletics training

handball-uebungen.de
Training Units and Exercises for Your Training !

Table of contents:

Introduction

Publishing information
1st English edition released on 09 Aug 2017
German original edition released on 18 Jan 2017

Published by: DV Concept
Editors, design, and layout: Jörg Madinger, Elke Lackner
Proofreading and English translation: Nina-Maria Nahlenz

ISBN: 978-3-95641-190-8

This publication is listed in the catalogue of the **German National Library.** Please refer to http://dnb.de for bibliographic data.

Handball Practice 11 – Extensive and diverse
athletics training

handball-uebungen.de
Training Units and Exercises for Your Training !

Introduction

Dear reader

Thank you for choosing a book of the handball-uebungen.de training guide series.

The present training units can support you in improving your team's handball-specific fitness, especially in terms of speed, speed endurance, and strength.

The strength training units focus on improving core stability with musculoskeletal and dynamic stabilization exercises. Stability plays an important role in handball, as it is crucial to a high physical performance and can prevent injuries.

Considering speed and speed strength, reflexive jumping power, short sprints, and speed endurance are especially important. These skills are essential for succeeding in handball.

The training units combine course strength trainings with short contests and handball-specific exercises, thus showing the possibilities for creating a diverse fitness training that is also fun for the team.

The present training units are designed for older youth teams and adult teams. Hence, certain physical requirements must be met. The exercises can also be used in the training of younger teams, however, you have to make sure that the difficulty level is appropriate for the younger players.

This book contains the following training units:

TU 1 – Series of shots with reflexive jumping power training (273) (★★★★)
This unit focuses on training the jumping power with handball-specific shooting exercises. After warm-up, a coordination run exercise, and a sprint contest, ball familiarization includes jumping and additional exercises with the ball. After the goalkeeper warm-up shooting, reaction time and jumping power are trained in two individual shooting exercises. A closing game completes this training unit.

Handball Practice 11 – Extensive and diverse
athletics training

handball-uebungen.de
Training Units and Exercises for Your Training !

TU 2 – Intensive speed strength/speed strength endurance training with various running directions (TU 279) (★★★★)

This athletics unit focuses on improving speed strength endurance. After warm-up and a short game, five athletics exercises train the various groups of thigh muscles by moving forwards, backwards, and to the side. This training unit is very intense and can thus be incorporated in preparation periods or season breaks.

TU 3 – Handball-specific endurance training with fast break movements (285) (★★★★)

This unit trains handball-specific endurance focusing on running and jumping exercises. After warm-up including a coordination run exercise, ball familiarization includes a passing and running course across the whole court. Goalkeeper warm-up shooting includes a series of 4 shots combined with a subsequent 2-on-2 fast break. The following endurance unit requires jumping exercises and playing 2-on-2 across the whole court alternately. This intense unit ends with a team exercise and a team fast break contest.

TU 4 – Intense athletics training for arms and legs (297) (★★★★)

This intense training unit focuses on athletics training. After warm-up including a game with high running intensity and a coordination run exercise, an athletics course is done. An additional jumping and strength exercise for the arms and a running exercise complete this training unit.

TU 5 – Handball-specific endurance training in game-like situations (319) (★★★)

This training unit contains a playful, handball-specific endurance unit. Each exercise is characterized by a high running intensity and is directly related to the handball game. After warm-up and ball familiarization as well as goalkeeper warm-up shooting, an endurance course is done. In this, two players have to accomplish a task as opponents. Which team is the first to score eight times? A sprint contest completes this intense training unit.

Handball Practice 11 – Extensive and diverse athletics training

handball-uebungen.de
Training Units and Exercises for Your Training!

1. Insight into the annual schedule

Annual schedule

The following points should be taken into consideration when creating your annual schedule:

- How many training units do I have (do not forget vacations, holidays, and the season schedule)?
- What do I want to achieve/improve this season?
- What goals should be achieved within a given concept (of the club, the association or federation)?
- What skills does my team have (do the individual players have)? You should continuously analyze and document the skills of your team so that you can make a target-performance comparison at a regular basis. The level of performance especially varies among young players. This has to be taken into consideration when training these teams. By making well-matched groups, you can optimize the performance of individual players in group training. You may also incorporate your own training units for certain performance groups or players with similar deficits in the annual schedule.

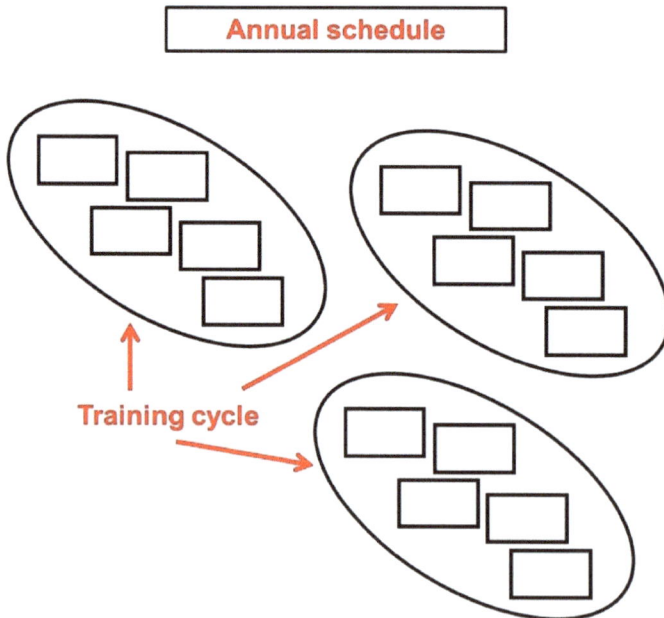

Annual schedule

Training cycle

Handball Practice 11 – Extensive and diverse
athletics training

handball-uebungen.de
Training Units and Exercises for Your Training !

Individual steps of the annual schedule:
- You may divide your annual schedule into special subsections.
- In the training of a youth team, you might want to apply the following structure:
  - End of season to summer vacations
  - Training during the vacations
  - Phase until beginning of next season
  - You may want to divide the season into a first and a second half (still keeping the vacations in mind).

You should then refine and elaborate these training phases step by step.
- Division of training phases into sections with part-specific objectives (monthly schedule, e.g.)
- Division into weekly schedules
- Planning of individual training units

The present training units are especially suitable for the preparation periods, but also for longer breaks between matches during the season.

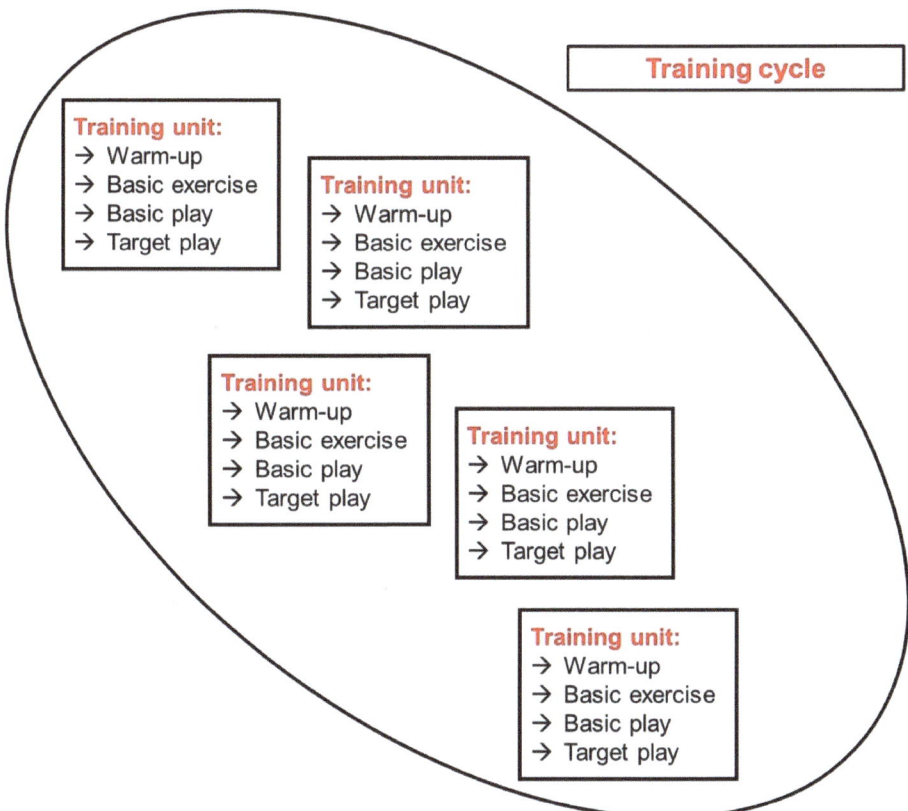

Training cycle

Training unit:
→ Warm-up
→ Basic exercise
→ Basic play
→ Target play

Training unit:
→ Warm-up
→ Basic exercise
→ Basic play
→ Target play

Training unit:
→ Warm-up
→ Basic exercise
→ Basic play
→ Target play

Training unit:
→ Warm-up
→ Basic exercise
→ Basic play
→ Target play

Training unit:
→ Warm-up
→ Basic exercise
→ Basic play
→ Target play

Handball Practice 11 – Extensive and diverse
athletics training

handball-uebungen.de
Training Units and Exercises for Your Training !

Creating well-structured training units

A clear structure is important for the annual schedule as well as for the planning of the individual training units.

- Work with parts (see monthly schedule). You should work on a special topic over a certain period of time, especially in the training of youth teams. That way, you can repeat exercises and make sure the players memorize the courses.
- Each training unit should have a clear training focus. Do not mix topics within a training unit, but make sure that each exercise has a well-defined objective.
- The players are corrected in accordance with the training unit's focus (when training the defense, defense actions are corrected and pointed out).

2. Structuring a training unit

The structure of training units focusing on endurance and athletics is often not comparable to the standard handball training unit with basic exercises, basic play, and target play.

There are, however, certain rules you should keep in mind when creating such a training unit.

Warm-up/activation:
Before each athletics training, the players must warm up thoroughly. Muscles and joint structures have to be sufficiently warm before starting with the athletics exercises.

Depending on the training requirements, you may include ball familiarization, goalkeeper warm-up shooting, or short games in the warm-up phase.

The main part may be a course or consist of a series of athletics exercises. Short contests can be motivating for the players.

The training unit should end with a cool-down phase including a closing game or a stretching and jogging phase.

Handball Practice 11 – Extensive and diverse athletics training

handball-uebungen.de
Training Units and Exercises for Your Training !

3. Roles/tasks of the coach

It is mainly the personality and the behavior of the coach that makes the training a success. Therefore, it is important to observe certain behavioral rules to guarantee a successful training. The coach's social skills have an impact as important as his expertise. Especially when training youth teams, the coach serves as a role model and may influence the development of the young players.

A coach should:
- describe the training and its objectives to his team at the beginning of the training unit.
- always speak loud and clear.
- talk from such a position that all players can hear his instructions and corrections.
- recognize and correct mistakes and give advice when correcting.
- mainly correct what is part of the training objective.
- point out and compliment on individual progress (give the player self-confidence).
- support and permanently challenge the players.
- always be a role model – during training and games, but also outside the court.
- come to training and games well-prepared and in a timely manner.

Especially when training youth teams:
- The coach should react to different physical preconditions. This is especially important when training athletics. The difficulty level should always match the players' level of performance. For heterogeneous groups, you might have to present a less difficult version for physically weaker players.
- Motivate the players to hang in, even if they face certain difficulties in the beginning.

Handball Practice 11 – Extensive and diverse athletics training

handball-uebungen.de
Training Units and Exercises for Your Training !

4. Training units

No.: 1	Series of shots with reflexive jumping power training (TU 273)		★★★★	90
Opening part		**Main part**		
X	Warm-up/Stretching	X	Offense/Individual		Jumping power
	Running exercise		Offense/Small groups	X	Sprint contest
	Short game		Offense/Team		Goalkeeper
	Coordination		Offense/Series of shots		
X	Coordination run		Defense/Individual	**Final part**	
	Strengthening		Defense/Small groups	X	Closing game
X	Ball familiarization		Defense/Team		Final sprint
X	Goalkeeper warm-up shooting		Athletics training		
			Endurance training		

★ : Low level (all youth and adult teams)	★ ★ : Medium level (youth teams under 15 years of age and adult teams)	★ ★ ★ : High level (youth teams under 17 years of age and adult teams)	★ ★ ★ ★ : Top level (competitive area)

Key:

✗   Cone

△1   Offense player

◯1   Defense player

▭   Small gym mat

▭   Large vaulting box

▬   Balance bench

▦   Ball box

●   Balloon

▦   Hurdle

Equipment required:
➔ 4 hurdles, 2 balance benches, 2 small gym mats, 10 cones, upper parts of 2 vaulting boxes, 1 balloon

Description:

This unit focuses on training the jumping power with handball-specific shooting exercises. After warm-up, a coordination run exercise, and a sprint contest, ball familiarization includes jumping and additional exercises with the ball. After the goalkeeper warm-up shooting, reaction time and jumping power are trained in two individual shooting exercises. A closing game completes this training unit.

The training unit consists of the following key exercises:
- Warm-up/Stretching (individual exercise: 10 minutes/total time: 10 minutes)
- Coordination run (10/20)
- Sprint contest (10/30)
- Ball familiarization (15/45)
- Goalkeeper warm-up shooting (10/55)
- Offense/Individual (10/65)
- Offense/Individual (15/80)
- Closing game (10/90)

Total training time: 90 minutes

Handball Practice 11 – Extensive and diverse
athletics training

handball-uebungen.de
Training Units and Exercises for Your Training !

No.: 1-1	Warm-up/Stretching	10	10

Course:

- The players independently crisscross the court with a handball. If two players meet, they do the following:
  - Exchange a high five with one hand
  - Shortly touch each other with the foot
  - Jump into the air and exchange a high five there
  - Jump into the air and bump into each other at chest level
  - Exchange handballs
- Upon the coach's whistle, two players exchange their handballs and keep running across the court afterwards.
- If the coach whistles twice, the players have to pass the ball to the wall, catch it again, and then keep running across the court.

All players do independent stretching exercises.

Handball Practice 11 – Extensive and diverse
athletics training

handball-uebungen.de
Training Units and Exercises for Your Training !

No.: 1-2	Coordination run	10	20

Setting:

- Position four hurdles (the first and third hurdle at maximum height, the second and fourth hurdle at minimum height), 10 cones, and the two balance benches (two or three to avoid a queue) as shown in the figure.

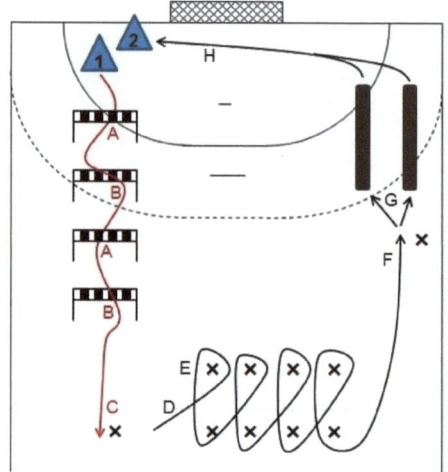

Course:

- 1 starts, crawls under the first hurdle (A), stands up immediately, and jumps over the second hurdle with both legs (B).
- At the third (A) and fourth hurdle (B), the course is repeated.
- After jumping over the fourth hurdle, 1 runs towards the backmost cone at a higher pace (C).
- Afterwards, 1 does a slalom run around the cones as shown in the figure (forward movement straight ahead (D), sidesteps to the right (E)) and finally runs towards the backmost cone at a higher pace (F).
- 1 chooses a balance bench, lies down on it face-down, and pulls himself to the other side using his arms only (lift feet) (G).
- At the end, 1 lines up for the next round again (H).
- Each player must do the exercise three times. Afterwards, the players may take a short break.
- In the second round, the courses are repeated highly dynamically and at full speed (also three times).

No.: 1-3	Sprint contest	10	30

Setting:

- Position three cone goals in the center as shown in the figure (with the goal in the middle being slightly further in the back).
- Make two teams. Each team stands in one of the diagonal corners.

Course:

- The defensive team decides which player starts the course (1).
- 1 steps forward and waits for the start (A).
- The attacking team may now decide which player (2) runs against 1 (B).
- 2 tries to run through one of the cone goals (C and E) without being touched by 1 (D).
- If he succeeds, the attacking team gets one point for each of the outer cone goals and two for the cone goal in the middle.
- As soon as all the attacking players have completed the course once (each attacking and each defending player has to run once), the teams switch tasks.
- Which team scores highest?

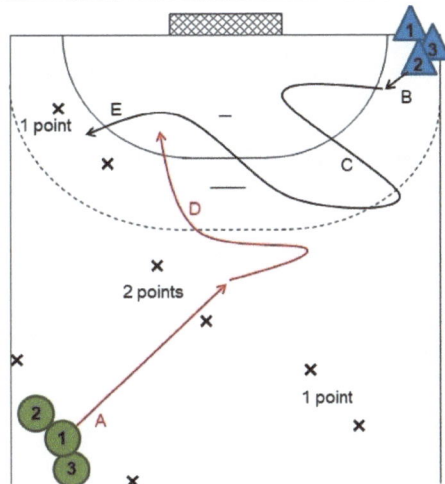

⚠ Both teams must communicate to make "ideal" pairs.

Handball Practice 11 – Extensive and diverse
athletics training

handball-uebungen.de
Training Units and Exercises for Your Training !

No.: 1-4	Ball familiarization	15	45

Setting:

- and serve as receivers.
- Put the upper part of a vaulting box on the floor for the jump shot extension.
- Put a small gym mat on the floor for landing during the Kempa extension.

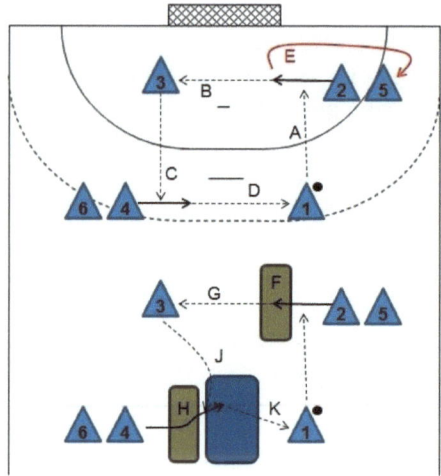

Course:

- starts and receives a pass from into his running path (A).
- passes the ball to while running (B).
- passes the ball into 's running path (C).
- passes the ball to while running (D) etc.
- After passing, and move back immediately and line up again (E).
- After several rounds, and are being replaced.

⚠ has to pass the ball directly without dribbling (B).

Jump shot extension:

- The passing remains as described above (A to E).
- After catching the ball (A), steps on the upper part of the vaulting box with his takeoff leg (F), immediately jumps again in a dynamic manner and passes the ball to doing a jump shot (G).

Kempa extension:

- The passing remains the same as described above (A to E).
- starts and jumps from the vaulting box with his takeoff leg (H), receives a pass from into his jump (J), and directly passes on the ball to while jumping (K).

⚠ At the beginning of the exercise, the players may catch the ball with both hands and pass it on with both hands during the jump.

Handball Practice 11 – Extensive and diverse
athletics training

handball-uebungen.de
Training Units and Exercises for Your Training !

| No.: 1-5 | Goalkeeper warm-up shooting | 10 | 55 |

Course for field players:

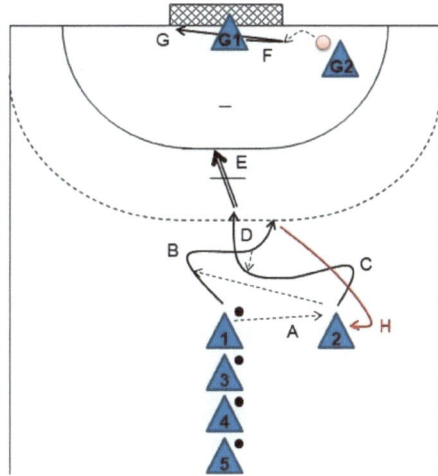

- **1** passes the ball to **2** (A) and clearly moves to the left.

- **2** passes the ball into **1**'s path in such a way that **1** can catch the ball while feinting the move to the left and then initiate a crossing to the right immediately (B).

- After his initial pass, **2** makes a running feint to the right (C), takes on the crossing of **1**, receives the ball (D) and makes a jump shot at the goal as instructed (top or bottom) (in the example, to the left) (E).

- After the crossing, **1** moves back immediately (H), takes on the next crossing of **3**, and the course starts over.

Course for the goalkeeper:

- The goalkeeper **G2** throws a balloon towards the goal which the goalkeeper **G1** has to bounce back before it touches the ground (F).

- The timing should be as follows: After bouncing the balloon back, the goalkeeper **G1** moves back to the center of the goal. After that, **1** can make his shot and the goalkeeper **G1** is able to save it (G).

⚠ The goalkeeper **G2** has to throw the balloon in such a way that the goalkeeper **G1** can reach it and that the shooting players are not interrupted in their shooting course.

⚠ The course has to be timed in such a way that the goalkeeper **G1** has to continuously reach the balloon and save the shot alternately.

Handball Practice 11 – Extensive and diverse
athletics training

handball-uebungen.de
Training Units and Exercises for Your Training !

No.: 1-6	Offense/Individual		10	65

Setting:

- Position the upper parts of two vaulting boxes as shown in the figure.

Course:

- **1** starts and does quick jumping jacks on the spot (A).

- **G** rolls, while **1** does the jumping jacks, the ball to the side (after 2 to 5 seconds) (B).

- This is the sign for **1** to start. Depending on which side the ball is rolled by **G**, **1** runs around the first cone:

  - o If **G** rolls the ball to the right (as shown in the figure), **1** runs around the first cone on the right (C).

  - o If **G** rolls the ball to the left, **1** runs around the first cone on the left.

- **1** runs across the vaulting box (D) and receives the ball there (E).

- Once he reaches the end of the vaulting box, **1** jumps, lands on his takeoff leg, and starts a jump shot at the goal immediately afterwards (F).

- **G** receives a new ball and the course starts over with **2** etc.

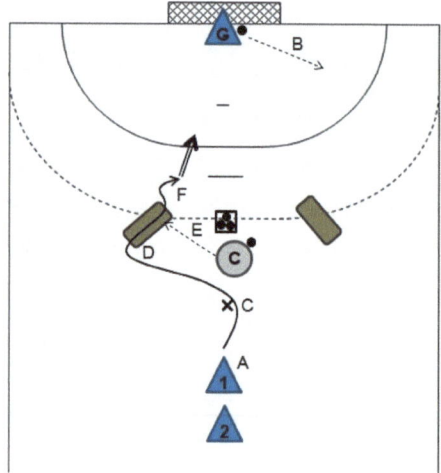

⚠ When **1** starts the jump shot (F), make sure that he only touches the floor for a short instance before starting the jump shot.

Handball Practice 11 – Extensive and diverse
athletics training

handball-uebungen.de
Training Units and Exercises for Your Training!

No.: 1-7	Offense/Individual	15	80

Setting:
- Put a small gym mat about 4-5 meters in front of the 9-meter line.
- Position two cones as shown in the figure.

Course:

- Standing on his left leg, 🔺1 (not included in the figure) starts the course on a small gym mat, jumps to the right on one leg, and straight into the air dynamically. Immediately after landing for the second time, 🔺1 jumps back to the left where he also jumps into the air dynamically (A and B).

- 🔺1 repeats this course until the coach Ⓒ whistles.

- Now, 🔺1 jumps dynamically forward on the leg he is currently standing on and receives a pass from Ⓒ into his jump (C). 🔺1 catches the ball in the air and lands on both legs.

- After landing, 🔺1 makes three steps towards the goal (without dribbling) and makes a jump shot at the goal on the 9-meter line over 🟢1, who serves as the passive block (D).

- After the initial action, 🔺1 starts a counter movement immediately, runs around the cone (E), receives the ball from Ⓒ into his running path, and makes a shot over 🟢1, who serves as the passive block (F).

- After the initial shot, 🟢1 immediately takes the position for the second shot (G).

- After the second shot, 🔺1 starts a counter movement immediately, runs around the backmost cone (H), receives a pass from Ⓒ into his running path and makes a shot over 🟢1, who serves as the passive block (J).

- After the second shot, 🟢1 immediately takes the position for the third shot (K).

- Afterwards, it is 🔺2's turn and 🔺1 becomes the new defensive player.

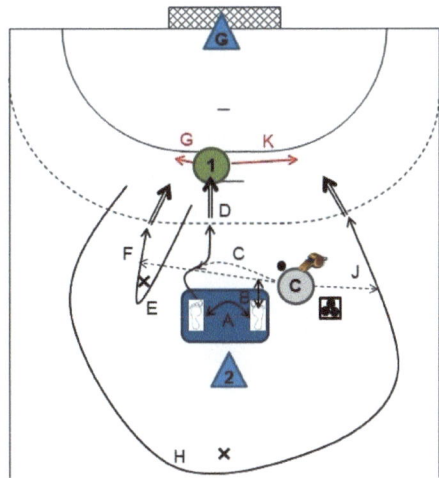

⚠️ The jumps on the gym mat must be carried out high and dynamically.

Handball Practice 11 – Extensive and diverse
athletics training

handball-uebungen.de
Training Units and Exercises for Your Training !

No.: 1-8	Closing game	10	90

Setting:
- Make two teams. Both teams play 6-on-6 against each other.
- Both teams play a 6:0 defense system.

Course:
- The teams must score a goal by simple crossing and subsequent shooting at the 9-meter line. If the attacking team scores a goal, they may start another attack at the center line.
- Which team scores highest? Define a task for the losing team before the game (carry the winners' bags at the next game, e.g.).

Notes:

_____

_____

_____

_____

_____

_____

_____

_____

_____

Handball Practice 11 – Extensive and diverse
athletics training

handball-uebungen.de
Training Units and Exercises for Your Training !

No.: 2	Intense speed strength/speed strength endurance training with various running directions (TU 279)	★★★★	90

Opening part		Main part			
X	Warm-up/Stretching		Offense/Individual		Jumping power
	Running exercise		Offense/Small groups		Sprint contest
X	Short game		Offense/Team		Goalkeeper
	Coordination		Offense/Series of shots		
	Coordination run		Defense/Individual		**Final part**
	Strengthening		Defense/Small groups		Closing game
	Ball familiarization		Defense/Team		Final sprint
	Goalkeeper warm-up shooting	X	Athletics training		
			Endurance training		

★ : Low level (all youth and adult teams)	★ ★ : Medium level (youth teams under 15 years of age and adult teams)	★ ★ ★ : High level (youth teams under 17 years of age and adult teams)	★ ★ ★ ★ : Top level (competitive area)

Key:

✖ Cone

1 Offense player

Small vaulting box

Coordination ladder

○ Hoop

Hurdle

Balance bench

Carpet tile

Equipment required:
➔ 1 coordination ladder
6 hoops, 2 hurdles, 2 small vaulting boxes, 4 balance benches, 10 cones, 1 carpet tile and 1 Deuser rubber band per team of two, 1 soccer ball

Description:

This athletics unit focuses on improving speed strength endurance. After warm-up and a short game, five athletics exercises train the various groups of thigh muscles by moving forwards, backwards, and to the side. This training unit is very intense and can thus be incorporated in preparation periods or season breaks.

The training unit consists of the following key exercises:
- Warm-up/Stretching (individual exercise: 10 minutes/total time: 10 minutes)
- Short game (10/20)
- Athletics training (15/35)
- Athletics training (15/50)
- Athletics training (15/65)
- Athletics training (15/80)
- Athletics training (10/90)

Total training time: 90 minutes

⚠ Most carpet stores sell carpet tiles. They often have remnants you can cut to length.

Handball Practice 11 – Extensive and diverse
athletics training

handball-uebungen.de
Training Units and Exercises for Your Training !

No.: 2-1	Warm-up/Stretching	10	10

Setting:

- Position cones (black) for the outer course.
- Arrange the inner course as shown in the figure.

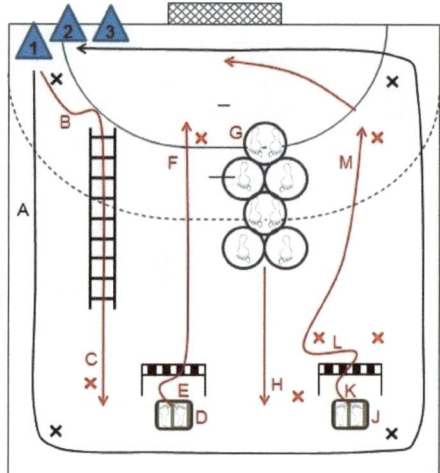

Course:

- ▲1 starts and runs the outer course at a relaxed pace (A).
- The other players start the course slightly delayed and run the outer course as well.
- After completing the outer course, ▲1 enters the inner course (B), runs through the coordination ladder with two quick footsteps per interspace (left and right), and afterwards speeds up on his way towards the cone (C).
- ▲1 stands on the small vaulting box (D), jumps down (E), and immediately jumps over the hurdle afterwards. After the hurdle, ▲1 speeds up and runs towards the cone (F).
- ▲1 jumps through the hoops as shown in the figure (jumps into the single hoop with both legs, jumps through the double hoops with one foot each (left and right), etc.) (G). The player leaves the hoops and runs towards the cone at a slightly higher speed (H).
- ▲1 stands on the small vaulting box (J), jumps down (K), and immediately jumps over the hurdle afterwards. After landing, ▲1 immediately runs to the left and around the left cone (in the next round, ▲1 runs around the right cone etc.) (L), and speeds up towards the cone (M).
- Afterwards, ▲1 runs the outer course again (A).

Overall course:

- Each player must do the exercise four times.
- The first two rounds, the players may run at a relaxed pace and the hurdles are low.
- In the following two rounds, the players must speed up and the hurdles are slightly higher.

No.: 2-2	Short game	10	20

Setting:
- Position four balance benches as shown in the figure. The seating surfaces must point towards the court (turned over by 90 degrees).
- Make two teams.
- The teams play soccer 2-on-2.
- The teams have to decide in which order their players are to enter the playing field.

Course:
- △1 and △2 play against ●1 and ●2 and try to score by kicking the ball against the seating surface of the balance bench (A, B, and C).
- If a team scores, the four players △1, △2, ●1, and ●2 must leave the playing field at their balance bench immediately (D) (give a high-five). They are not allowed to enter the game again while leaving the playing field. One new player per balance bench is allowed to enter the playing field then (E).
- Now, △3 and △5 play against ●3 and ●5, until a team scores the next goal. The players then also leave the playing field at their balance bench and so on.
- The players waiting outside to be substituted do both push-ups and sit-ups alternately during the waiting periods.

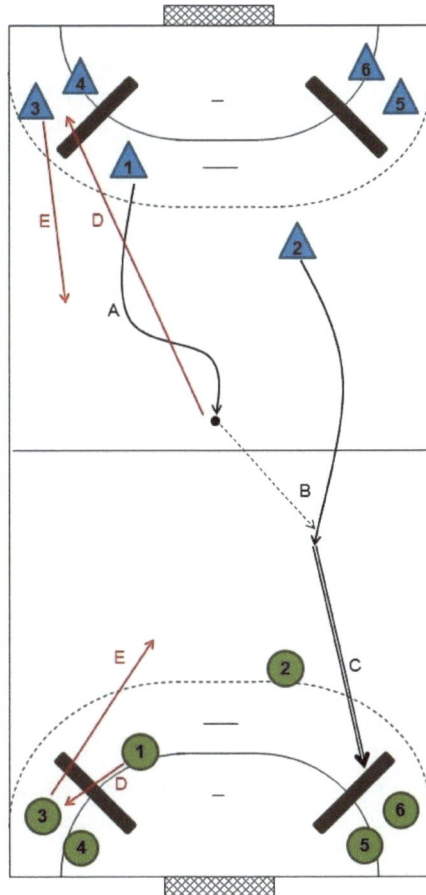

⚠ For larger groups, play 4-on-4 (two players per balance bench).

Handball Practice 11 – Extensive and diverse athletics training

handball-uebungen.de
Training Units and Exercises for Your Training !

No.: 2-3	Athletics training	15	35

Setting:

- Define a start line and position a cone at a distance of about 20 meters.
- The players make pairs; each pair has a Deuser rubber band and a carpet tile.
- ![1] wraps the Deuser band around his hips. The second player stands behind him on the carpet tile and grabs the band with both hands.

Course:

- On command, the players in the front start to pull carefully (A).
- After a few meters, they speed up to a sprint (B) and keep up that speed for about 10 meters.
- Before reaching the cones, the players must slow down considerably and run around the cone (C).
- As soon as the player in the back has been pulled around the cone and is back in line with ![1], the pulling player speeds up to a sprint again (D) and keeps up that speed for about 10 meters.
- The players then slow down and come to a halt after the finish line (E).
- Afterwards, the players switch tasks and repeat the course.
- Once both players have done the running part, they do 10 slow and 10 fast jumping jacks on the spot to loosen their muscles.

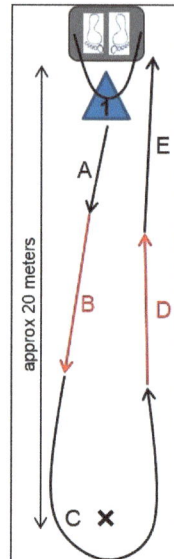

Overall course:

- Each player alternately does the course (pulling, being pulled, jumping jacks) four times.
- Afterwards, the players stand on the goal line and run towards the other side of the court speeding up. They have to reach their maximum speed at the center line.
- They then run back to the start line while speeding up.

Handball Practice 11 – Extensive and diverse athletics training

handball-uebungen.de
Training Units and Exercises for Your Training!

Course after the exercise:
- The players run from goal line to goal line at a relaxed pace for about 4-5 minutes.

⚠ In the beginning and after the turns, the players must pull and speed up slowly so that the player being pulled can stay on the carpet tile.

⚠ The player in the back may squat or slightly bend his knees (figure 1).

⚠ The player in the back must strongly flex his muscles so that he does not fall off the carpet tile when being pulled by 1.

(Figure 1)

No.: 2-4	Athletics training	15	50

Setting:
- Define a start line and position a cone at a distance of about 20 meters.
- The players make pairs; each pair has a Deuser rubber band and a carpet tile.
- Both players stand face-to-face. 1 wraps the Deuser band around his hips. The second player stands on the carpet tile and grabs the band with both hands.

Course:
- On command, the players in the front start to pull carefully while moving backwards (A).
- After a few meters, they speed up to a sprint (B) and keep up that speed for about 10 meters.
- Before reaching the cones, the players must slow down considerably and run around the cone (C).
- As soon as the player in the back has been pulled around the cone and is back in line with 1, the pulling player speeds up to a sprint again (D) and keeps up that speed for about 10 meters.
- The players then slow down and come to a halt after the finish line (E).
- Afterwards, the players switch tasks and repeat the course.
- Once both players have done the running part, they do 10 slow and 10 fast jumping jacks on the spot to loosen their muscles.

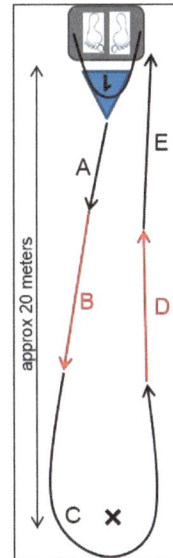

Overall course:

- Each player alternately does the course (pulling, being pulled, jumping jacks) four times.
- Afterwards, the players line up on the goal line, sprint towards the second cone on command (F), sprint backwards towards the first cone (G), sprint forwards again towards the third cone (H), etc., until they reach the fifth cone (J).

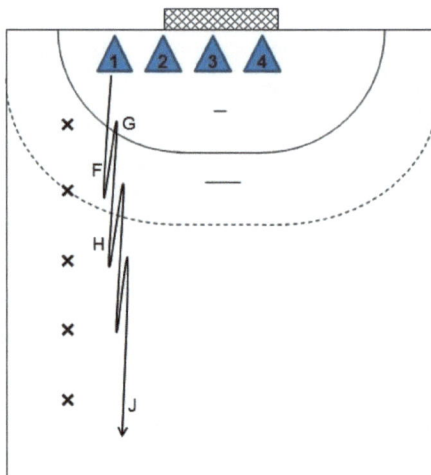

Course after the exercise:

- The players run at a relaxed pace from goal line to goal line for about 4-5 minutes.

⚠ The players running backwards must start with small steps tiptoeing. As soon as they have gained speed, they may increase the length of their steps.

⚠ The players running backwards must make sure they do not step on the carpet tile.

Handball Practice 11 – Extensive and diverse
athletics training

handball-uebungen.de
Training Units and Exercises for Your Training !

No.: 2-5	Athletics training	15	65

Setting:

- Define a start line and position a cone at a distance of about 15 meters.
- The players make pairs; each pair has a Deuser rubber band and a carpet tile.
- 1 stands sideways in front of the other player, who stands on the carpet tile, and wraps the Deuser band around his hips. The player in the back grabs the band with both hands.

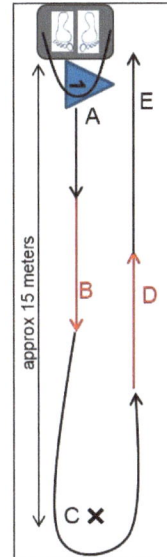

Course:

- On command, the players in the front start to pull carefully while sidestepping (A).
- After a few meters, they speed up considerably (B) and keep up that speed for about 5-6 meters.
- Before reaching the cones, the players must slow down considerably and run around the cone (C).
- As soon as the player in the back has been pulled around the cone and is back in line with 1, the pulling player makes a turn of 180° and again speeds up considerably (D) before coming to a halt after the finish line (E).
- Afterwards, the players switch tasks and repeat the course.
- Once both players have done the running part, they do 10 slow and 10 fast jumping jacks on the spot to loosen their muscles.

Overall course:

- Each player alternately does the course (pulling, being pulled, jumping jacks) four times.
- Afterwards, the players sprint towards the first cone (F), run around it, and quickly sidestep through the other cones (G) before they finally sprint forwards to the last cone (H).

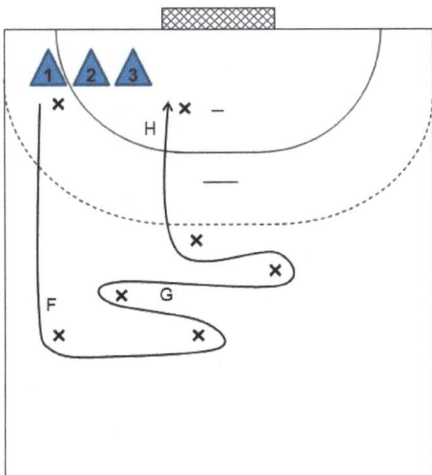

⚠ The sidestepping part is very intense.

Course after the exercise:

- The players run from goal line to goal line at a relaxed pace for about 4-5 minutes.

Handball Practice 11 – Extensive and diverse
athletics training

handball-uebungen.de
Training Units and Exercises for Your Training !

No.: 2-6	Athletics training	10	75

Setting:

- Define a start line and position a cone at a distance of about 25 meters.
- The players make pairs; each pair has a carpet tile.
- ▲ stands behind the player standing on the carpet tile. Both players face the center of the court (A).

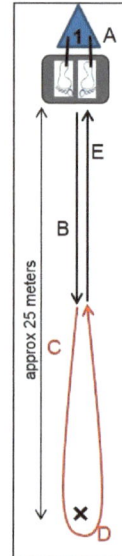

Course:

- On command, all the players in the back start pushing the players on the carpet tiles forward (B).
- Once they have gone half the way, the pushing players make a sidestep and sprint towards the center line (C).
- The players run around the cone quickly and speed up once again (D).
- Meanwhile, the players on the carpet tiles have made a turn of 180° and are now being pushed back over the finish line by the other players (E).
- Afterwards, the players switch tasks and repeat the course.

Course after the exercise:

- The players run from side line to side line at a relaxed pace for about 4-5 minutes.

⚠ The players on the carpet tiles must strongly flex their muscles so that they can be pushed by the other players.

Handball Practice 11 – Extensive and diverse
athletics training

handball-uebungen.de
Training Units and Exercises for Your Training !

No.: 2-7	Athletics training	15	90

Setting:
- Position four cones as shown in the figure.
- The players make pairs; each pair has a Deuser rubber band and a carpet tile.
- 1 wraps the Deuser band around his hips. The second player stands behind him on the carpet tile and grabs the band with both hands.

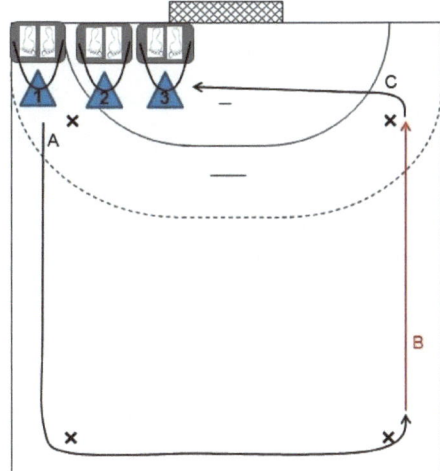

Course:
- Each pair starts the course independently.
- 1 starts to pull carefully and jogs around the cones while pulling the player standing behind him on the carpet tile (A).
- After the third cone, 1 sprints towards the fourth cone (B), then slows down and keeps jogging at a relaxed pace (C).
- 1 repeats the course four times without taking a break, always sprinting between the third and the fourth cone.
- After four rounds, the two players switch positions and repeat the course.

⚠ The pulling players should try to jog as long as possible (A and C).

Course after the exercise:
- The players run from goal line to goal line at a relaxed pace for about 1-2 minutes and cool down stretching afterwards.

Notes:

_____

_____

_____

Handball Practice 11 – Extensive and diverse athletics training

handball-uebungen.de
Training Units and Exercises for Your Training !

No.: 3	Handball-specific endurance training with fast break movements (TU 285)	★★★★	90

Opening part		Main part			
X	Warm-up/Stretching	X	Offense/Individual		Jumping power
	Running exercise		Offense/Small groups		Sprint contest
	Short game		Offense/Team		Goalkeeper
	Coordination		Offense/Series of shots		**Final part**
X	Coordination run		Defense/Individual		
	Strengthening		Defense/Small groups		Closing game
X	Ball familiarization		Defense/Team		Final sprint
X	Goalkeeper warm-up shooting		Athletics training	X	Team exercise
		X	Endurance training		

★: Low level (all youth and adult teams)	★ ★: Medium level (youth teams under 15 years of age and adult teams)	★ ★ ★: High level (youth teams under 17 years of age and adult teams)	★ ★ ★ ★: Top level (competitive area)

Key:

✕ Cones (two colors)

△ 1 Offense player

● 1 Defense player

Ball box

Coordination ladder

Foam noodles (foam beams)

Hurdle

○ Hoop

● Medicine ball

Equipment required:
→ 5 foam beams, 7 red cones, 11 black cones, 4 hurdles, 6 hoops, 1 coordination ladder, 2 medicine balls, 2 ball boxes with sufficient number of handballs, 1 whistle

Description:

This unit trains handball-specific endurance focusing on running and jumping exercises. After warm-up including a coordination run exercise, ball familiarization includes a passing and running course across the whole court. Goalkeeper warm-up shooting includes a series of 4 shots combined with a subsequent 2-on-2 fast break. The following endurance unit requires jumping exercises and playing 2-on-2 across the whole court alternately. This intense unit ends with a team exercise and a team fast break contest.

The training unit consists of the following key exercises:
- Warm-up/Stretching (individual exercise: 10 minutes/total time: 10 minutes)
- Coordination run (10/20)
- Ball familiarization (10/30)
- Goalkeeper warm-up shooting (10/40)
- Endurance course (25/65)
- Team exercise (10/75)
- Offense/Individual (15/90)

Total training time: 90 minutes

No.: 3-1	Warm-up/Stretching	10	10

Course:

- Two players crisscross the court with a handball and easily pass the ball back and forth (short and long passes).
- At the same time, they try to steal the ball from another group. However, they have to keep passing their own ball and each player is only allowed to dribble twice. If they win another ball, they have to play passes with two balls at a time. The team who lost their ball does 10 quick jumping jacks and has to try to regain another ball afterwards.
- The players have to change their running moves constantly (forwards, backwards, sidesteps).

⚠ A player is only allowed to dribble the ball two times in a row. After that, he must pass the ball.

The players perform stretching exercises together.

Handball Practice 11 – Extensive and diverse athletics training

handball-uebungen.de
Training Units and Exercises for Your Training !

No.: 3-2	Coordination run	10	20

Setting:
- Position cones (seven red and seven black cones), hurdles, hoops, and foam beams as shown in the figure.

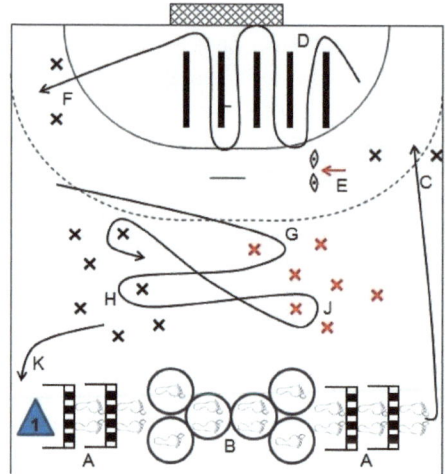

Course:
- ▲1 starts right in front of the hurdle. He jumps over the two hurdles with both legs (A), jumps through the hoops as shown in the figure (B), and immediately jumps over the next two hurdles with both legs.
- After landing, ▲1 sprints to the side immediately and runs through the cone goal (C).
- Afterwards, ▲1 does a slalom run through the foam beams moving sideways as fast as possible (D) while looking in the direction of the cones behind the foam beams (E). At the end of the foam beam course, he shortly sprints through the cone goal (F).
- Eventually, he runs a slalom around the ten cones in the center. The players have to switch between red (G) and black (H) and red (J) cones etc. They are not allowed to run around the same cone twice.
- After the 10th cone, ▲1 directly starts the next round (K).

Overall course:
- Each player does the course twice at a moderate pace.
- Afterwards, he takes a short stretching break.
- Then the course is repeated two more times at maximum pace.

handball-uebungen.de
Training Units and Exercises for Your Training !

No.: 3-3	Ball familiarization	10	30

Course:

- 🔺1 passes the ball to the goalkeeper 🔺G1 (A) and starts to run forward dynamically.

- The goalkeeper 🔺G1 passes the ball back into 🔺1's running path immediately (B).

- 🔺2 starts dynamically and receives the pass from 🔺1 into his running path (C).

- After playing the pass, 🔺1 stands at the center line (D).

- While running, 🔺2 passes the ball to the other goalkeeper 🔺G2 (E) and runs around the cone (F). The goalkeeper 🔺G2 passes the ball back into his running path (G).

- 🔺3 starts and receives a pass from 🔺2 into his running path (H).

- After playing the pass, 🔺2 stands at the center line (J).

- After he finished the course, 🔺3 lines up again.

- 🔺4 starts the same course slightly delayed. Time the start in such a way that the players only have to wait at the center line for a little while before they receive the next pass (C and G).

⚠ The players should run at full speed and pass the ball they received as fast as possible.

No.: 3-4	Goalkeeper warm-up shooting	10	40

Setting:

- Position a coordination ladder in front of the goal.
- For each round, there are four players holding a handball and ready to start the series of shots.

Course:

- The goalkeeper **G1** starts the course jumping (A) through the coordination ladder while doing jumping jacks (B). Once he reaches the end, he runs into the goal and turns around.

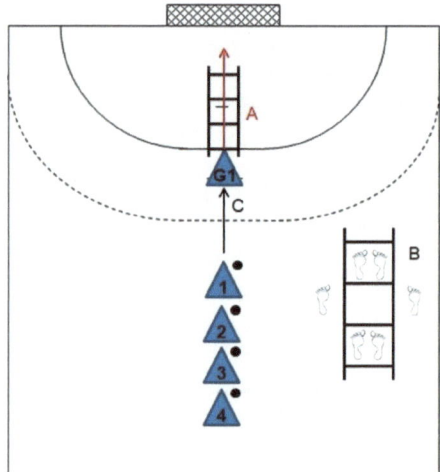

- As soon as the goalkeeper **G1** has reached the ideal position, the four shooting players start the series of shots (C):

  - **1** shoots at the top left corner.
  - **2** shoots at the top right corner.
  - **3** shoots at the bottom left corner.
  - **4** shoots at the bottom right corner.

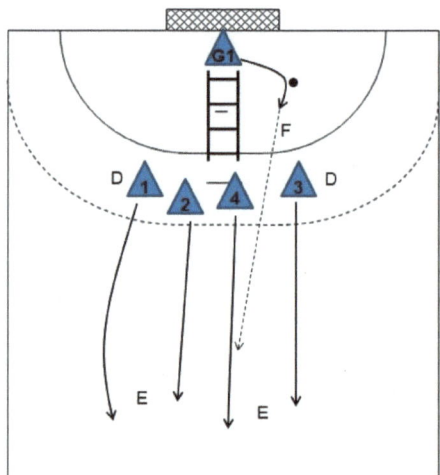

- After shooting, the players remain in the zone between the 6- and the 9-meter line (D).

- After **4** has shot, all four players start to run a fast break (E).

- **1** and **3** now play 2-on-2 against **2** and **4** in order to shoot at goal on the other side.

- After the last shot, the goalkeeper **G1** immediately fetches one of the four thrown balls and passes it into the running path of one of the four players (F). The goalkeeper **G1** may freely chose the player he passes the ball to.

- Afterwards, the course is repeated with the next four shooting players etc.

No.: 3-5	Endurance course	25	65

Setting:

- If the court has an outer track, position the five hurdles there as shown in the figure. If there is no outer track, position the hurdles at the level of the center line.
- Put two medicine balls next to the hurdles.

Course on the court:

- ▲1 and ▲2 play 2-on-2 against ●1 and ●2.
- Both teams may play freely and try to shoot at the goal (A, B, and C).
- If a team scores, the goalkeeper immediately starts over by playing a pass (D); there is no throw-off at the center line.
- If a player is fouled between the 6- and 9-meter line while playing towards the goal, the attacking player is immediately awarded a 7-meter penalty.
- The four players keep on playing 2-on-2 until ▲3 and ▲4 have finished their exercises.
- Both teams count the shots they missed (the players of each team add up the shots they missed).

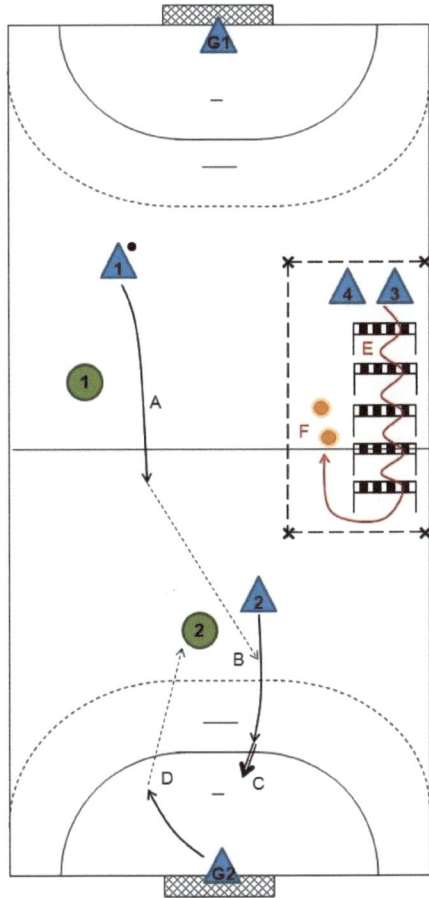

Handball Practice 11 – Extensive and diverse
athletics training

handball-uebungen.de
Training Units and Exercises for Your Training !

Course for the players at the hurdles:

- 3 and 4 jump over the five hurdles one after the other with both legs and without any additional jumps between the hurdles (E) (figure 1 and 2).

(Figure 1)

- Afterwards, 3 and 4 take the medicine balls and do the following exercise five times in a row:

    o They take the medicine ball with both hands and squat down (figure 3).

    o Then, they dynamically jump from the squatting position into a straight jump and throw the medicine ball in the air (figure 4).

(Figure 2)

- 3 and 4 repeat the course (jumping over the hurdles and throwing the medicine ball in the air) five times.

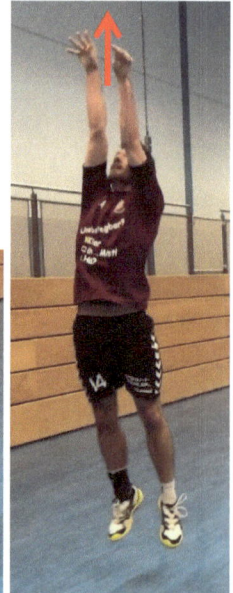

Overall course:

- 1 and 2 keep on playing 2-on-2 against 1 and 2 as long as it takes 3 and 4 to complete the exercise five times.

- Afterwards, the team who shot the most goals leaves the court and does (for each shot the team missed) 10 push-ups and 10 sit-ups. Then, they wait until it is their turn to do the hurdle course.

(Figure 3)   (Figure 4)

- Each team has to do the 2-on-2game two times at most. If they still have not won after that, they are being replaced anyway. In that case, they have to do the exercises for the missed shots from both rounds outside the court (push-ups and sit-ups).

- Each player has to do the whole course (2-on-2, hurdles, and medicine ball) twice.

Handball Practice 11 – Extensive and diverse
athletics training

handball-uebungen.de
Training Units and Exercises for Your Training !

No.: 3-6	Team exercise	10	75

Setting:
- The players, each holding a handball, stand in a circle.

Course:
- The players receive a task and have 30 seconds to find a solution by communicating as a team.
- After 30 seconds, the coach whistles (A) and the players must accomplish a task.
- The players may try three times to accomplish the respective task. If they fail to accomplish the task three times, the must do 10 quick jumping jacks, e.g.

Tasks for 12 players:
- The players must pass their handballs simultaneously for 20 seconds (B). Exactly three passes **always should** be bounce passes (C).
- Two players must exchange their balls by passing, so do the next two players, and so on, until all players have exchanged balls. When training an odd number of players, one of them has to pass twice. While passing, the players are not allowed to talk to each other anymore.
- One ball is passed from player to player by kicking while the other balls must be passed conventionally at the same time. The player currently kicking the ball is not allowed to hold a ball simultaneously. The players are only allowed to hold the ball for two seconds. Then, they must play a pass. The ball serving as the soccer ball has to be passed on immediately (1 contact with the ball only).

⚠ During the 30 seconds before the coach's whistle (A), the players must decide precisely on how to accomplish the task.

Handball Practice 11 – Extensive and diverse
athletics training

handball-uebungen.de
Training Units and Exercises for Your Training !

No.: 3-7	Offense/Individual	15	90

Setting:
-   Put a ball box next to each goal.

Course:
-   **1** starts a fast break from the corner and receives a long pass from the goalkeeper **G1** into his running path (A).
-   **1** shoots at the goal while running (B).
-   While **1** makes his shot, **1** starts a fast break from the corner (C) and receives a long pass from the goalkeeper **G2** into his running path (E).
-   **1** starts a counter movement directly after his shot (D) and tries to prevent **1** from shooting.
-   **1** shoots (F), starts a counter movement immediately (G), and tries to prevent **2** from making a fast break.

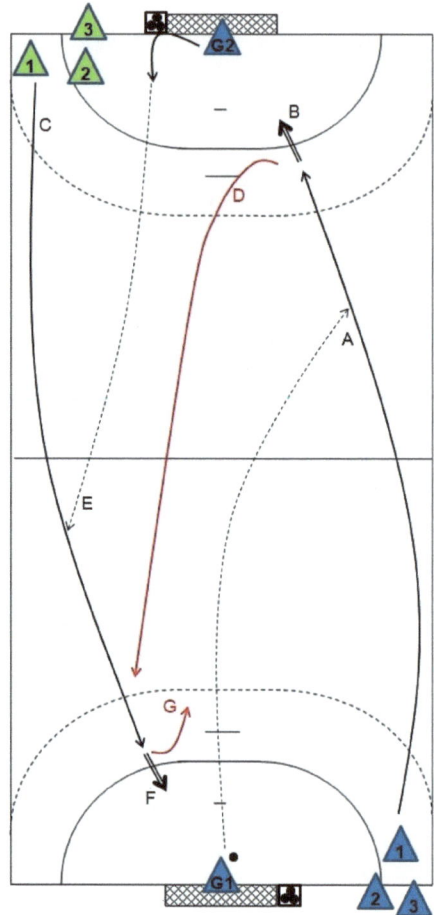

Overall course:
-   Each player must do the course three times on each side (six shots). The players must count the shots they missed themselves.
-   The winning team does two push-ups and two sit-ups per shot missed.
-   The losing team does five push-ups and five sit-ups per shot missed.

⚠ Make sure that the players doing the subsequent fast breaks only start (C) once the other player has completed his shot (B).

Handball Practice 11 – Extensive and diverse athletics training

handball-uebungen.de
Training Units and Exercises for Your Training !

No.: 4	Intense athletics training for arms and legs (TU 297)		★★★★	90

Opening part		Main part			
X	Warm-up/Stretching		Offense/Individual		Jumping power
	Running exercise		Offense/Small groups		Sprint contest
X	Short game		Offense/Team		Goalkeeper
	Coordination		Offense/Series of shots		
X	Coordination run		Defense/Individual		**Final part**
	Strengthening		Defense/Small groups		Closing game
	Ball familiarization		Defense/Team		Final sprint
	Goalkeeper warm-up shooting	X	Athletics training		
			Endurance training		

★: Low level (all youth and adult teams)	★★: Medium level (youth teams under 15 years of age and adult teams)	★★★: High level (youth teams under 17 years of age and adult teams)	★★★★: Top level (competitive area)

Key:

✖ Cone

🔺1 Offense player

🟢1 Defense player

Large safety mat

Balance bench

Foam noodles (foam beams)

Parallel bars

Roller board

🟠 Basketball

Equipment required:
➔ 3-4 basketball baskets, 6-8 basketballs, if available (otherwise handballs), 8 foam beams, parallel bars, 2 roller boards, 2 large safety mats, 5 balance benches, timer, whistle

Description:

This intense training unit focuses on athletics training. After warm-up including a game with high running intensity and a coordination run exercise, an athletics course is done. An additional jumping and strength exercise for the arms and a running exercise complete this training unit.

My thanks go to Jannik and Marius for their enthusiastic support.

The training unit consists of the following key exercises:
- Warm-up/Stretching (individual exercise: 10 minutes/total time: 10 minutes)
- Short game (15/25)
- Coordination run (10/35)
- Athletics course (30/65)
- Athletics training (15/80)
- Running exercise (10/90)

Total training time: 90 minutes

No.: 4-1	Warm-up/Stretching	10	10

Course:

- Make two groups.
- Each team is assigned a leader. The leader runs ahead and shows exercises which the other players must copy.
- Upon the coach's whistle, the next player becomes the leader and shows exercises.
- The players perform stretching exercises together.

No.: 4-2	Short game	15	25

Setting:

- Four players each stand under a basketball basket with two basketballs.
- Define a throw-off (penalty) line for each basketball basket.

⚠ The game is very exhausting, as the players have to move permanently.

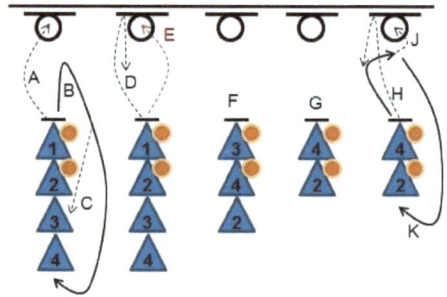

Course:

- 🔺 **1** starts the course and shoots at the basket from the throw-off line (A).
  - ○ If 🔺**1** scores right away, he fetches his own ball (B), passes it to 🔺**3** (C), and lines up again.
  - ○ If 🔺**1** does not score right away (H), he may fetch his ball and try again (J). While doing this, he is allowed to freely change his position.
- As soon as 🔺**1** has shot at the basket, 🔺**2** steps forward and immediately makes a shot at the basket as well (E).
  - ○ If he does not score right away either, he may also fetch his ball and try to shoot at the basket.
- If 🔺**2** manages to score before 🔺**1** (E), 🔺**1** is disqualified.
  - ○ 🔺**1** still fetches his ball however and passes it to 🔺**3**.
  - ○ 🔺**2** quickly fetches the ball after shooting at the basket (E), passes it to 🔺**4**, and lines up again (F).

- The course is repeated until only two players are left (G).
- Now, a scoring player (H and J) fetches his ball quickly, runs towards the throw-off line immediately and shoots at the basket again (K), until one of the two players scores before the other one. The player who scores first gets a point and the course starts over.

Idea of the game:

- The players always play 2-on-2 against each other.
- If the player shooting second (2) scores before the player who shot first (1), 1 is disqualified.
- Afterwards, 2 and 3 play against each other.
- If the player shooting first always scored first, the course would continue forever, as no player could ever be disqualified.
- If the player shooting second scores before the player who shot first, this player is disqualified.

Overall course:

- Each group of 4 continues to play until a player has scored five points. Then, there will be new groups of 4 with the first two winners and the last two losers each making new groups of 4. Repeat the course until another player has scored five times.

Handball Practice 11 – Extensive and diverse
athletics training

handball-uebungen.de
Training Units and Exercises for Your Training !

No.: 4-3	Coordination run	10	35

Basic course:
- The players do the following running or jumping exercises over 3-4 lanes (half of the court):

Athletic hopping (figure 1):
- The payers jump up forwards and land on the same leg. The movement is done with both legs alternately. Elbows and knees are bend in a right angle.

(Figure 1)   (Figure 2)

Long jump running (figure 2):
- The players change feet during each jump (jumping up with the left, landing with the right foot, jumping up again with the right foot immediately). The players should make a long jumping movement.

⚠ The players have to jump up (figure 1) and forward (figure 2) dynamically and have to push themselves up vigorously with the tips of their toes.

Double jump running:
- The players continuously jump up with the left leg twice and the right leg twice (change of routine 1x (left leg) – 2x (right leg) – 2x (left leg) – 1x (right leg) and so on).

Partner skipping (figure 3):
- First, the players do several dynamic skipping moves on the spot individually.
- For partner skipping, the player in the back holds the hips of the player in front of him, who then does skipping moves being held back. The player in the back lets go after 2-3 seconds independently. The player in the front now uses the additional energy and speeds up across a distance of 10-15 meters (figure 4).

(Figure 3)

Handball Practice 11 – Extensive and diverse
athletics training

handball-uebungen.de
Training Units and Exercises for Your Training !

⚠ When speeding up, the player should lift his knees considerably without being thrown off balance.

(Figure 4)

No.: 4-4	Athletics course	30	65

Setting:
- Position parallel bars, 8 foam beams, 2 roller boards, 2 large safety mats as shown in the figure (figure 1).

General course:
- There are two players at each position doing the respective exercise alternately (one player takes a break, the other does the exercise).
- The players must do the exercises in the order shown in the figure.

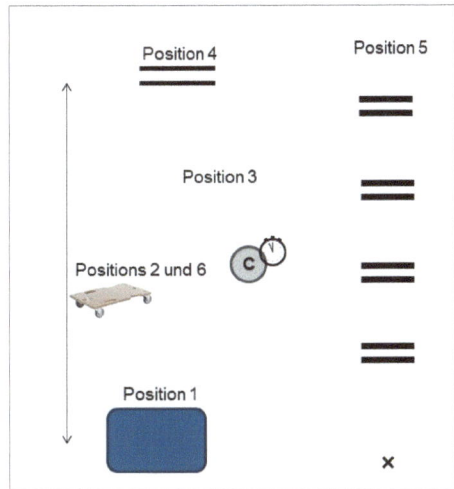

Position 4   Position 5

Position 3

Positions 2 und 6   C

Position 1

×

(Figure 1)

Time:
- Player 1 does the exercise for one minute.
- During a break of 10 seconds, the next player gets ready to do the exercise.
- Player 2 does the exercise for one minute.
- During a break of 10 seconds, the players change the position.
- And so on.
- After the players have completed each exercise once, they may take a break of two minutes. After that, the course starts over a second time.

Handball Practice 11 – Extensive and diverse
athletics training

handball-uebungen.de
Training Units and Exercises for Your Training !

Position 1 (large safety mats):
Setting:
- Put two large safety mats on top of each other.

Course:
- The players stand in front of the large safety mats (figure 2), jump up forward dynamically and land in a stable sitting position (figure 3).
- You may use a cone to mark the starting line (at a distance of about 1 meter in front of the mats).

(Figure 2)

(Figure 3)

Position 2 and position 6 (roller board):
Setting:
-   Provide a roller board and define an area for rolling.

Course at position 2:
-   The players lie down on a roller board face-down (figure 4) and push themselves forward dynamically using both hands at the same time. When doing that, they must lift their upper body considerably (figure 5).

Course at position 6:
-   The players lie down on a roller board face-down (figure 6) and push themselves forward dynamically using both hands alternately (crawl move). When doing that, they must lift their upper body considerably.

(Figure 4)

(Figure 5)

(Figure 6)

Handball Practice 11 – Extensive and diverse
athletics training

handball-uebungen.de
Training Units and Exercises for Your Training !

Position 3 (intermuscular jumping coordination):
Course:
- The players do a deep lunge (figure 7), dynamically jump up from this position (push themselves up with both legs at the same time) (figure 8), and land in a deep lunge with both legs at the same time again and without changing the position of their legs.
- Change the side after five jumps and so on.

(Figure 7)

(Figure 8)

⚠ The players have to make sure that their knees are in line with their feet. In figure 7, both knees are turned inwards too far.

Position 4 (parallel bars):
Course:
- The player is in the support position on the parallel bars (figure 9).
- He lifts his legs and spreads them across the bars to the left and the right without touching the bars (figure 10).
- Afterwards, he closes his legs, does the support position again (figure 9), and does a dip (figure 11), and so on.

(Figure 9)

(Figure 10)

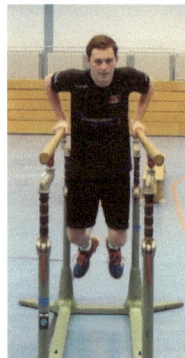
(Figure 11)

⚠ The exercise should be done slowly and continuously. Make sure the players' backs remain straight.

Handball Practice 11 – Extensive and diverse
athletics training

handball-uebungen.de
Training Units and Exercises for Your Training !

Position 5 (foam beam course):
Setting:
- Position the foam beams in such a way that they can be crossed with two long jumps.

Course:
- The player crosses the large gap with two long jumps (A) and makes a high jump over the two foam beams. (B).
- After the last foam beam, he sprints towards the cone (C).
- Afterwards, the player runs back at a fast pace and repeats the course.

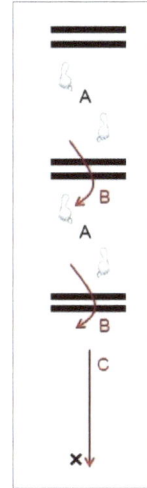

No.: 4-5	Athletics training	15	80

Setting:
- Put five balance benches next to each other with each interspace being about 1 meter.

Course 1:
- The players stand on the bench (figure 1), jump down with both legs, immediately jump up again dynamically (reflexively), and land on the next bench. (A).
- The players repeat the exercise at the next three benches.
- When standing on the last bench, the players jump down with both legs and sprint towards the cone (C).
- Each player must do five courses.

(Figure 1)

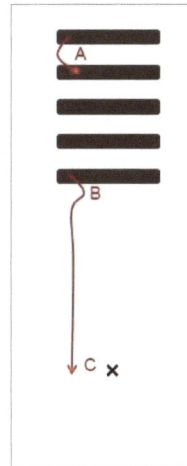

(Figure 2)

Course 2:
- One player does the wheelbarrow next to the first bench, the other player holds up his legs (figure 3).
- The player crosses the benches on his hands (figure 4) until he is next to the fifth bench. Afterwards, the exercise is repeated with the other player.

⚠ The players must avoid a swayback (actively flex their abdominal muscles).

Higher difficulty level:
- The player does a push-up between the benches (figure 5). While he does the push-up, the player holding his legs should slightly bend his knees to prevent him from getting a swayback.

(Figure 3)   (Figure 4)   (Figure 5)

Handball Practice 11 – Extensive and diverse
athletics training

handball-uebungen.de
Training Units and Exercises for Your Training !

No.: 4-6	Running exercise	10	90

Course:

- The players run next to each other from goal line to goal line at a relaxed pace (A).

- Once the coach Ⓒ whistles (B), **1** and **2** start the course. Both start to sprint until they reach the other players in their running direction again (C and D). The other players keep running at a relaxed pace (A).

- Once **1** and **2** have reached the other players again, they slow down and run along with the others. As soon as the coach Ⓒ whistles again, it is the next two players' turn.

- The course is repeated until all players have done the exercise twice.

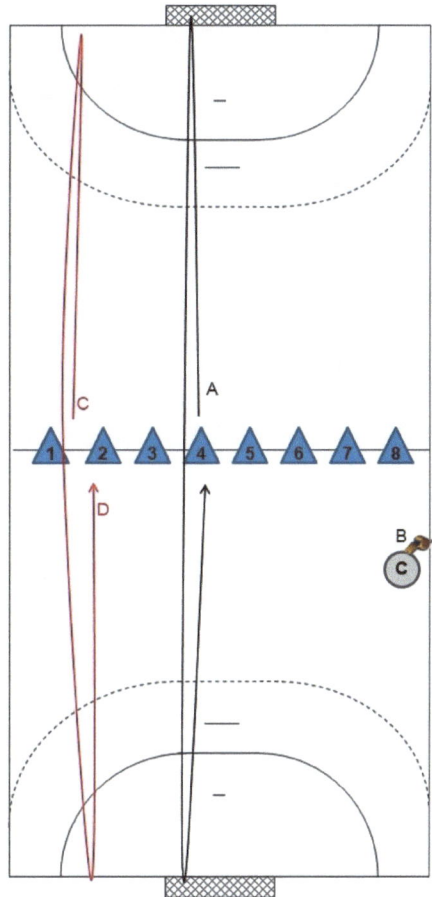

Notes:

_____

_____

_____

_____

Handball Practice 11 – Extensive and diverse athletics training

handball-uebungen.de
Training Units and Exercises for Your Training !

No.: 5	Handball-specific endurance training in game-like situations (TU 319)	★★★	90

Opening part		Main part			
X	Warm-up/Stretching		Offense/Individual		Jumping power
	Running exercise		Offense/Small groups	X	Sprint contest
	Short game		Offense/Team		Goalkeeper
	Coordination		Offense/Series of shots		
	Coordination run		Defense/Individual		**Final part**
	Strengthening		Defense/Small groups		Closing game
X	Ball familiarization		Defense/Team		Final sprint
X	Goalkeeper warm-up shooting		Athletics training		
		X	Endurance training		

★: Low level (all youth and adult teams) | ★★: Medium level (youth teams under 15 years of age and adult teams) | ★★★: High level (youth teams under 17 years of age and adult teams) | ★★★★: Top level (competitive area)

Key:

✖ Cone

🔺1 Attacking player

🟢1 Defense player

🟦 Small gym mat

Ball box

Large vaulting box

Hurdle

Balance bench

◯ Hoop

Equipment required:
➔ 10 cones, 2 hurdles, 1 balance bench, 6 hoops, 3 small gym mats, 4 large vaulting boxes, 2 ball boxes with 20 handballs

Description:
This training unit contains a playful, handball-specific endurance unit. Each exercise is characterized by a high running intensity and is directly related to the handball game. After warm-up and ball familiarization as well as goalkeeper warm-up shooting, an endurance course is done. In this, two players have to accomplish a task as opponents. Which team is the first to score eight times? A sprint contest completes this intense training unit.

The training unit consists of the following key exercises:
- Warm-up/Stretching (individual exercise: 10 minutes/total time: 10 minutes)
- Ball familiarization (10/20)
- Goalkeeper warm-up shooting (10/30)
- Endurance course (50/80)
- Sprint contest (10/90)
Training unit total time: 90 minutes

Handball Practice 11 – Extensive and diverse
athletics training

handball-uebungen.de
Training Units and Exercises for Your Training !

No.: 5-1	Warm-up/Stretching	10	10

Course:

- Each player independently dribbles across the court.
- The players have to change their running moves and dribble constantly (forwards, backwards, sidesteps, hopping, jump shots).
- Depending on how often the coach whistles, the players have to do the following exercises:
  - o One whistle: The players try to score a basketball basket as fast as possible and afterwards run into the center circle.
  - o Two whistles: The players try to hit the goalpost from the 6-meter line as fast as possible and afterwards run into the center circle.
  - o Three whistles: The players throw the ball straight into the air and have to turn around three times. They must not drop the ball afterwards. If they catch the ball after the third turn, the players run into the center circle.
- The last three players each have to do five quick jumping jacks.
- Between the exercises, the players keep running across the court.
- The players perform stretching exercises individually/together.

Handball Practice 11 – Extensive and diverse
athletics training

handball-uebungen.de
Training Units and Exercises for Your Training !

No.: 5-2	Ball familiarization	10	20

Setting:

- Position 10 cones, six hoops, and 1 small gym mat as shown in the figure.
- The players spread out behind the backmost cones (at least two players per cone). Two players (▲1 and ▲3) have a ball.
- The coach Ⓒ has some extra balls.

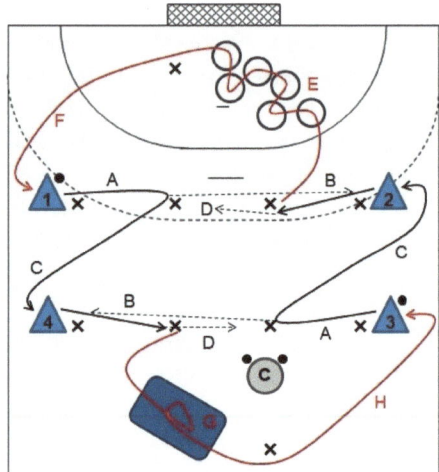

Course:

- ▲1 and ▲3 start the course simultaneously, make a piston movement towards the cone in the front (A), and pass the ball into the running path of ▲2 and ▲4 (B).
- After the pass, they move back and line up at the next position (C).
- ▲2 and ▲4 also make a piston movement towards the cone in the front and pass the ball into the running path of the next player on the other side (D).
- After the pass, ▲2 and ▲4 each do an additional exercise:
   - ▲2 runs through the hoop course at a fast pace, touching the ground only one time per hoop (E), runs around the cone, and lines up again (F).
   - ▲4 does a somersault on the gym mat (G), runs around the cone and lines up again (H).
- The course is continuously repeated.
- If a player loses a ball, the coach Ⓒ quickly passes a new one.

⚠ The players must do the additional exercise (E and G) quickly so that passing in the center is not delayed or even interrupted. Adjust the distance to the two cones for the additional exercises to the number of players.

Handball Practice 11 – Extensive and diverse athletics training

handball-uebungen.de
Training Units and Exercises for Your Training !

No.: 5-3	Goalkeeper warm-up shooting	10	30

Before the action:

- Before the exercise starts, the coach decides which player will be acting in the subsequent action (▲4 in the example) and gives him a sign what to do next in such a way that the goalkeeper cannot see it.

Course of action 1 (small figure):

- ▲1 starts and shoots at the goal as instructed (top, middle, bottom) (A).

- ▲2 starts the course slightly delayed so that the goalkeeper faces a series of shots.

- And so on.

- After shooting, the players quickly line up on the goal line (B).

Course of subsequent action:

- As soon as the last player makes his shot, the other players start running from the goal line towards the center line (D)

- ▲6 turns to the right immediately after his shot (C) and runs towards the center line as well (E).

- The player the coach appointed before the exercise (▲4) sprints at full speed, holding up his arm in such a way that the goalkeeper can see it.

- After the last shot (C), the goalkeeper ▲G1 fetches the ball as fast as possible (F) and passes it over the other players into the running path of ▲4 (G).

- ▲4 freely shoots at the opposite goal at the 9-meter line.

- Afterwards, the players repeat the course on the other side.

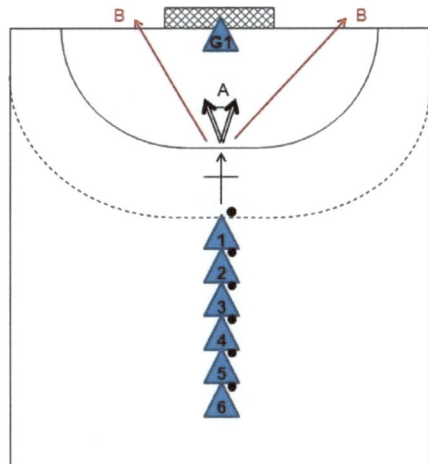

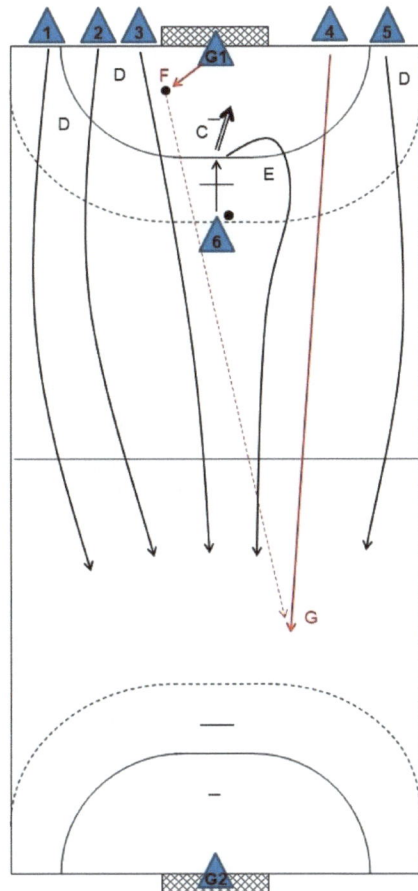

Handball Practice 11 – Extensive and diverse
athletics training

handball-uebungen.de
Training Units and Exercises for Your Training !

⚠ The other players must run at such a pace that 🔵4 can overtake several meters after the center line so that the goalkeeper 🔵G1 can play his pass.

No.: 5-4	Endurance course	50	80

Setting:

- Line up eight hoops outside the court. Position two differently colored cones in front of it.
- For the course, position the following items in the center of the court:
  - Position two hurdles (A), a balance bench (B), two large vaulting boxes (C), five hoops (D), and four cones in the center of the court as shown in the figure.
  - Put 2-3 small gym mats in the center (E).
- For the series of shots, position the following items in each half of the court:
  - One cone in the center, one cone on each wing position, one large vaulting box, two cones on the HL/HR positions, one ball box with ten balls.
- Prepare a reward for the winning team to motivate the players.

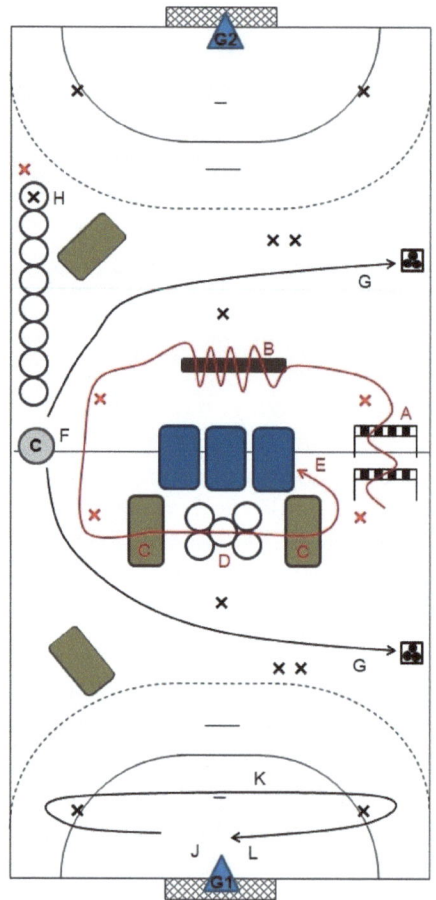

(Figure 1)

Handball Practice 11 – Extensive and diverse
athletics training

handball-uebungen.de
Training Units and Exercises for Your Training !

Basic course:

- Make two teams. Each team has to have a goalkeeper (goalkeeper G1 and goalkeeper G2).
- One player of each team comes to the coach (F). The other players do the course in the center (A to E)

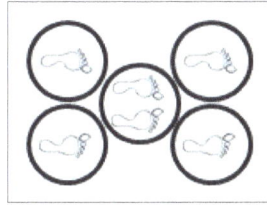
(Figure 2)

Course in the center:

- The players jump over the two hurdles with both legs (A).
- Then, they jump over the balance bench with one leg (B).
- They jump up on the vaulting box (C), jump down on the other side, jump through the hoops as shown in the figure (figure 2), and jump over the second vaulting box (D).
- Afterwards, they turn to the left towards the gym mats (E):
  - o On the gym mats, they do 10 push-ups and 10 sit-ups.
- The course is repeated until one of the shooting players has accomplished his task.

Course for the shooting players:

- The coach (c) shows the 1st shooting card to both players simultaneously (F).
- The players memorize the task.
- On command, the players start running towards their ball box (G) and accomplish their task. This is also the sign for the players in the center to start their course (A to E).
- As soon as one of the two players has accomplished his shooting exercise, all players stop their current action.
  - o The players in the center quickly fetch the balls.
  - o The player who has accomplished his task first may put his cone into the first hoop (H).
- The next course starts as soon as there are 10 balls in each ball box again. Two new players come to the coach (c), receive the next shooting card, and the course starts over with the new task.
- The players repeat the course until one team can put their cone into the eighth hoop. This team wins the overall course.
- If the eight shooting cards have been used and there is still no winner, the coach shuffles the cards and the players repeat the course until one team has eight points.

Handball Practice 11 – Extensive and diverse
athletics training

handball-uebungen.de
Training Units and Exercises for Your Training !

Tasks for the two goalkeepers between the shooting exercises after a player has accomplished his task:
- Five push-ups (J).
- Sprint around the cones once (K).
- Do sit-ups until the next two players come to the coach ⓒ (L) to receive a new task.

⚠ If it takes the shooting players too long to accomplish a task, the coach ⓒ must react and simplify the task.

⚠ The shooting players have to use the balls from their ball box first. If a box is empty, they may take a ball from the court, but have to run back to the ball box first, touch it, and start the next try from there.

⚠ After the shooting task, the players must fetch the balls quickly so that there will not be a too long break between the courses.

Shooting card 1 – Course:
- Take a ball from the ball box (A).
- Run around the cone and make a STEM SHOT at the goal from behind the 9-meter line (B).
- Fetch a new ball after the shot and keep shooting until you have accomplished the task (C).

Task:
- Shoot three goals in a row without missing the goal once.
- Over the line = missed shot.

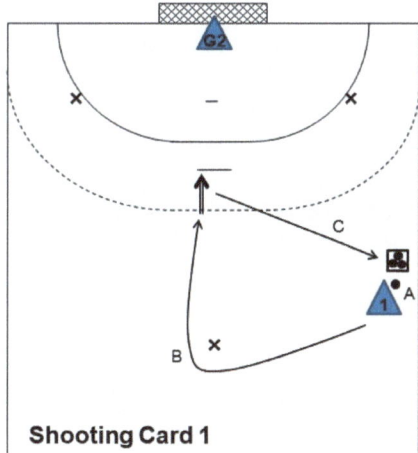

Shooting Card 1

Cutting edge--

Shooting card 2 – Course:
- Take a ball from the ball box (A).
- Run around the cone and shoot at the goal from the left wing position (B).
- Fetch a new ball after the shot and keep shooting until you have accomplished the task (C).

Task:
- Shoot four goals. One shot MUST be a BANANA SHOT or a SPIN SHOT.
- Over the line = missed shot.

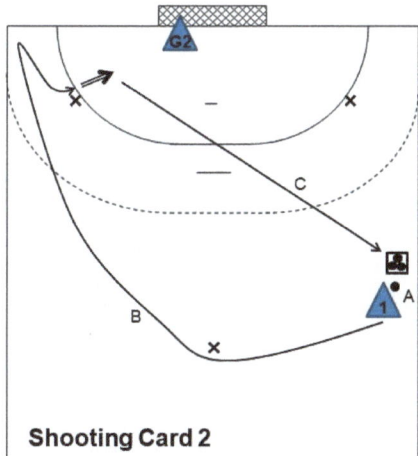

Shooting Card 2

Cutting edge--

Shooting card 3:

Course:
- Take a ball from the ball box (A).
- Run around the cone and shoot at the goal from behind the 9-meter line (B).
- Fetch a new ball after the shot and keep shooting until you have accomplished the task (C).

Task:
- Shoot six goals.
- Over the line = missed shot.

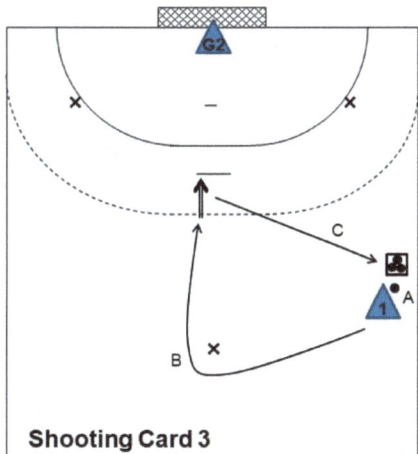

Shooting Card 3

Shooting card 4 – Course:
- Take a ball from the ball box (A).
- Run around the cone and shoot at the goal from the right wing position (B).
- Fetch a new ball after the shot and keep shooting until you have accomplished the task (C).

Task:
- Shoot four goals. One shot MUST be a BANANA SHOT or a SPIN SHOT.
- Over the line = missed shot.

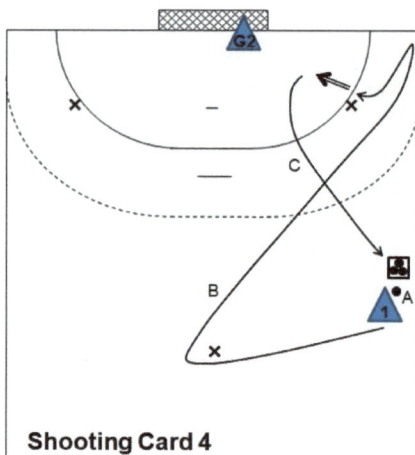

Shooting Card 4

Cutting edge---

Shooting card 5 – Course:
- Take a ball from the ball box (A).
- Run around the cone and make a JUMP SHOT at the goal from behind the 9-meter line (B).
- Fetch a new ball after the shot and keep shooting until you have accomplished the task (C).

Task:
- Shoot six goals. One goal MUST be shot by BOUNCING THE BALL.
- Over the line = missed shot.

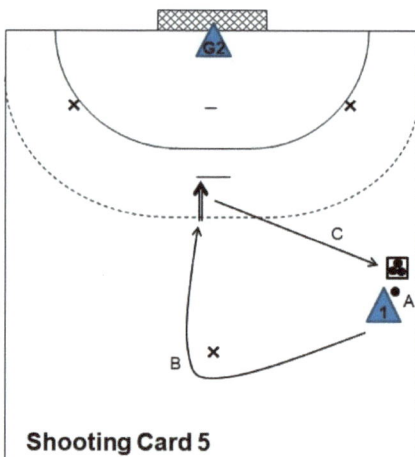

Shooting Card 5

Cutting edge---

Shooting card 6 – Course:
- Take a ball from the ball box (A).
- Run around the cone, pass the ball against the vaulting box, catch it again (B), and shoot at the goal from the 9-meter line.
- Fetch a new ball after the shot and keep shooting until you have accomplished the task (C).

Task:
- Shoot four goals. You must NOT dribble once you caught the ball.
- Over the line = missed shot.

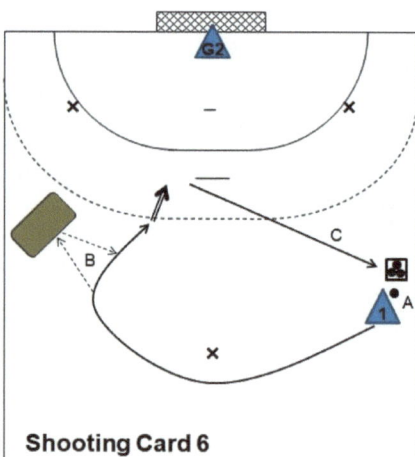

Shooting Card 6

Shooting card 7 – Course:
- Take a ball from the ball box (A).
- Run around the cone, dribble the ball forward when passing the cone, catch it, and shoot at the goal without dribbling again (B).
- Fetch a new ball after the shot and keep shooting until you have accomplished the task (C).

Task:
- Shoot four goals. One goal MUST be shot by BOUNCING THE BALL.
- Over the line = missed shot.

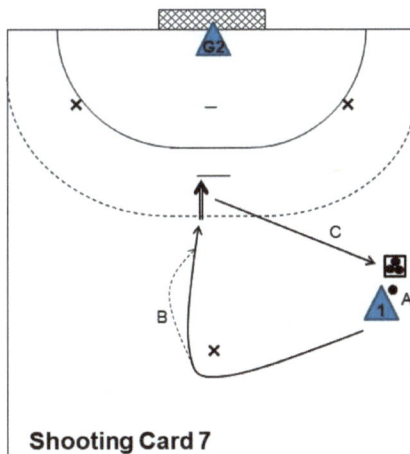

Shooting Card 7

Cutting edge--

Shooting card 8 – Course:
- Take a ball from the ball box (A).
- Run around the cone, catch the ball before the two cones, make a running feint with three steps (right/left or left/right), and shoot at the goal (B).
- Fetch a new ball after the shot and keep shooting until you have accomplished the task (C).

Task:
- Shoot four goals.
- Over the line = missed shot.

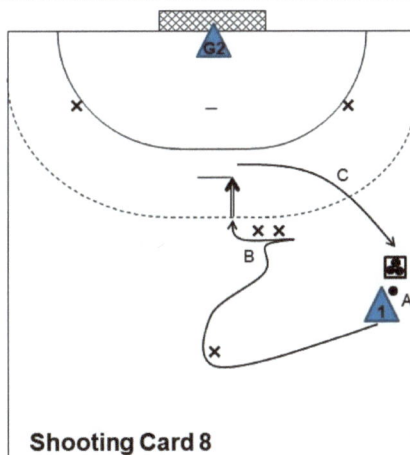

Shooting Card 8

Cutting edge--

No.: 5-5	Sprint contest		10	90

Setting:

- Make teams of three.
- For each team, position four cones as shown in the figure.

Course:

- On command, one player per team starts the course.
    - o He sprints forward towards the second cone (A).
    - o He runs backwards towards the first cone (B).
    - o He runs forward towards the fourth cone (C).
    - o He then runs backwards to the third cone (D).
    - o He eventually exchanges a high five with the player (E) who repeats the course on the other side (F).
- Each player sprints twice.
- Which team has crossed the goal line after the sixth sprint first?

2nd course:

- The players dribble while doing the course.

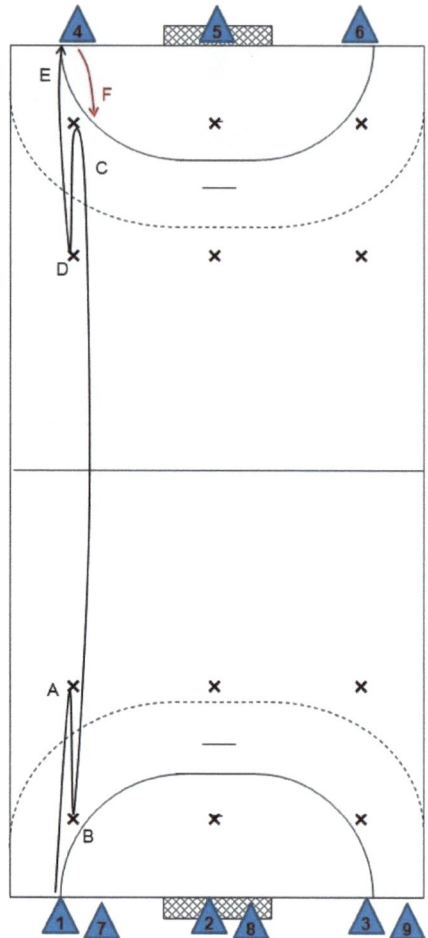

Notes:

_____

_____

_____

_____

_____

Handball Practice 11 – Extensive and diverse
athletics training

handball-uebungen.de
Training Units and Exercises for Your Training !

5. About the editor

JÖRG MADINGER, born in Heidelberg (Germany) in 1970

July 2014 (further training): 3-day coaching workshop: "Basic components of goalkeeper training", held by the German Handball Association (Deutscher Handballbund, DHB)
Lecturers: Michael Neuhaus, Renate Schubert, Marco Stange, Norbert Potthoff, Olaf Gritz, Andreas Thiel, Henning Fritz

May 2014 (further training): 3-day coaching further training during the VELUX EHF Final4, held by the German Handball Coaching Association (Deutsche Handball Trainer Vereinigung, DHTV)/DHB
Lecturers: Jochen Beppler (DHB coach), Christian vom Dorff (DHB referee), Mark Dragunski (coach of TUSEM Essen, Germany), Klaus-Dieter Petersen (DHB coach), Manolo Cadenas (coach of the Spanish national team)

May 2013 (further training): 3-day coaching further training during the VELUX EHF Final4, held by the DHTV/DHB
Lecturers: Prof. Dr. Carmen Borggrefe (University of Stuttgart, Germany), Klaus-Dieter Petersen (DHB coach), Dr. Georg Froese (sports psychologist), Jochen Beppler (DHB base camp coach), Carsten Alisch (young talents' hockey coach)

Since July 2012: A-License, DHB

Since February 2011: Handball club trainings, coaching (training and competitive areas)

November 2011: Foundation of the Handball Specialist Publishing Company (Handball Fachverlag) (handall-uebungen.de, Handball Practice and Special Handball Practice)

May 2009: Foundation of the handball online platform handball-uebungen.de

2008-2010: Youth coordinator and youth coach, SG Leutershausen (Germany)

Since 2006: B-License

Editor's note
In 1995, a friend convinced me to join him in coaching a handball youth team (male, under 13 years of age).

This was the beginning of my career as a team handball coach. Ever since I enjoyed working as a coach and had high requirements concerning my exercises. Soon, the standard pool of exercises wasn't enough for me anymore and I started to modify and develop drills myself.

Today, I coach a broad range of youth and adult teams with different performance levels and adjust my training units to the individual needs of the teams.

A few years ago, I started selling my exercises and drills online at handball-uebungen.de. Since, in handball training, there is a tendency towards a general athletic training that focuses on coordination work – especially in the training of youth teams –, a large number of my games and exercises can be applied to other sports as well.

Get inspired by the various game concepts, be creative, and rely on your own experiences!

Yours sincerely,
Jörg Madinger

Handball Practice 11 – Extensive and diverse
athletics training

handball-uebungen.de
Training Units and Exercises for Your Training !

6. Further reference books published by DV Concept

From warm-up to handball team play – 75 exercises for every handball training unit

By making your training units more diverse, you can increase the players' motivation, since you consistently offer new approaches to improve and refine familiar movement sequences. In this book, you will find inspiring exercises you can apply during each phase of your everyday team handball training – from warm-up and goalkeeper warm-up shooting to the common contents of the main phase and the closing games. Each exercise is illustrated and described in an easy, comprehensible manner. Specific notes give you tips on what you need to be aware of.

This book deals with the following key subjects:

Warm-up:
- Basic warm-up
- Short warm-up games
- Sprint contests
- Coordination
- Ball familiarization
- Goalkeeper warm-up shooting

Basic exercises, basic play, and target play:
- Offense/series of shots
- General offense
- Fast throw-off
- 1st and 2nd wave
- Defensive action
- Closing games
- Endurance

At the end of this book, you will find an entire methodological training unit. The objective of this training unit is to improve shooting and quick decision-making under pressure.

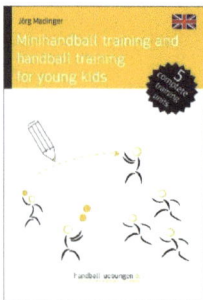

Minihandball training and handball training for young kids (5 training units)

Minihandball training and handball training for young kids is different from handball training for older players and considerably different from handball training for competitive players. During their first contact with "handball", kids should be familiarized with the ball in a playful way. They should be taught that being active, doing sports, playing together, and even playing against each other is fun.

This book contains a short introduction to handball for kids and young children and its special characteristics as well as example exercises which help to make your training units interesting and more diverse.

Following this, there are five complete training units of different difficulty levels that focus on the basic handball techniques (dribbling, passing, catching, shooting, and defending in a game with opponents). The kids are playfully introduced to the subsequent handball-specific basics. At the same time, particular attention is payed to general physical experience and the development of coordination skills.

The exercises are illustrated and described in an easy, comprehensible manner. They can be immediately integrated in every training unit. By using the given training variants, you can easily adjust the difficulty level of the training units to the respective target group. The variants should also encourage you to modify and further develop the exercises to make each training unit a new and more diverse experience for the children.

Handball Practice 11 – Extensive and diverse
athletics training

handball-uebungen.de
Training Units and Exercises for Your Training !

Competitive games for your everyday handball training – 60 exercises for each age-group

Handball needs quick and correct decisions in each game situation. This can be trained playfully and diversely through handball-specific games. These 60 exercises are divided into seven categories and train the playing skills.

The book contains the following contents:
- Team ball variants
- Team play with different targets
- Tag games
- Sprint and relay race games
- Ball throwing and transportation games
- Games from other types of sports
- Complex closing game variants

The exercises are illustrated and described in an easy, comprehensible manner. They can be immediately integrated in every training unit. Various difficulty levels, additional notes, and possible variations allow for adjustment to each age group.

For further reference and e-books visit us at:

www.handball-uebungen.de

www.ingramcontent.com/pod-product-compliance
Lightning Source LLC
Chambersburg PA
CBHW042130080426
42735CB00001B/27